ELEPHANTS
From Trunk to Tail

Lucy Sackett Smith

PowerKiDS
press
New York

Published in 2010 by The Rosen Publishing Group, Inc.
29 East 21st Street, New York, NY 10010

First Edition

Editor: Nicole Pristash
Book Design: Kate Laczynski
Photo Researcher: Jessica Gerweck

Photo Credits: Cover, pp. 1, 12–13 © www.istockphoto.com/Chuck Babbitt; p. 5 © Peter Johnson/Corbis; p. 7 Larry Dale Gordon/Getty Images; p. 9 Gallo Images-Heinrich van den Berg/Getty Images; p. 11 Wolfgang Bayer/Getty Images; p. 15 Stan Osolinski/Getty Images; p. 17 Winfried Wisniewski/Getty Images; p. 19 Jeffrey Conley/Gettty Images; p. 21 © www.istockphoto.com/Ewan Chesser.

Library of Congress Cataloging-in-Publication Data

Smith, Lucy Sackett.
  Elephants : from trunk to tail / Lucy Sackett Smith. — 1st ed.
      p. cm. — (Mighty mammals)
  Includes index.
  ISBN 978-1-4042-8102-8 (library binding) — ISBN 978-1-4358-3261-9 (pbk.) — ISBN 978-1-4358-3262-6 (6-pack)
  1. Elephants—Juvenile literature. I. Title.
  QL737.P98S644 2010
  599.67—dc22
                                  2008055084

Manufactured in the United States of America

CONTENTS

A Huge Animal...4

Where Do Elephants Live?.............................6

Wonderful, Useful Trunks 8

What Kind of Elephant Is That?..................10

Mighty Facts 12

Mothers in Charge 14

Cute Calves..16

Big Eaters 18

Who Would Hunt an Elephant?..................20

Elephants in Danger 22

Glossary..23

Index 24

Web sites 24

A Huge Animal

Elephants are Earth's largest land animals. Big elephants commonly weigh around 14,000 pounds (6,350 kg). That is how much 200 10-year-old kids weigh! Elephants are very strong. In some places, people have trained these powerful **mammals** to carry heavy loads.

Size is not the only thing that makes elephants special, though. These huge animals are smart as well. In fact, **scientists** now think elephants are some of the smartest animals around. Elephants are also known for their big ears and long **trunks**. Elephants use their trunks for many things, such as eating, drinking, and picking up objects.

Elephants travel in groups while searching for food and water.

Where Do Elephants Live?

Elephants live in Africa and Asia. Scientists put African elephants into two groups. African forest elephants live in the thick forests of central and western Africa. African bush elephants are found on Africa's **savannas**. These animals, also known as savanna elephants, are the biggest elephants.

Wild Asian elephants live in the forests of South Asia and Southeast Asia. There are also thousands of Asian elephants that have been trained to work for people. Many of these elephants pull heavy logs in the forests of Thailand and India. Elephant trainers, called mahouts, have trained Asian elephants for over 4,000 years.

Workers in Thailand have trained these Asian elephants to carry logs. Elephants can carry very heavy loads.

Wonderful, Useful Trunks

Elephants are known for their interesting trunks. A trunk is really an extra long nose and an upper lip. Elephants breathe and smell through their trunks, just as humans do through their noses. Since their trunks are so long, elephants can raise their trunks out of the water to breathe when the elephants swim.

Elephants drink by sucking water into their trunks and spraying the water into their mouths. They use their trunks to spray dust over themselves, too. This keeps bugs away from them. To let other elephants know that there is danger, elephants raise their trunks and make loud noises.

An elephant's trunk is very useful. This elephant is using its trunk to take a shower!

What Kind of Elephant Is That?

The different kinds of elephants may look the same, but they have many differences. African elephants have two bendable parts, known as fingers, at the ends of their trunks. Asian elephants have only one finger. Male and female African elephants have big teeth, called tusks. Generally, only male Asian elephants have tusks.

You can also tell the different kinds of elephants apart by their ears. Indian elephants have smaller ears than African elephants. African forest elephants have large, round ears. African bush elephants have ears that are shaped like Africa. Asian elephants are the second largest. African forest elephants are the smallest.

Elephants often use one tusk more than the other. They use their tusks for digging, lifting, and sometimes fighting.

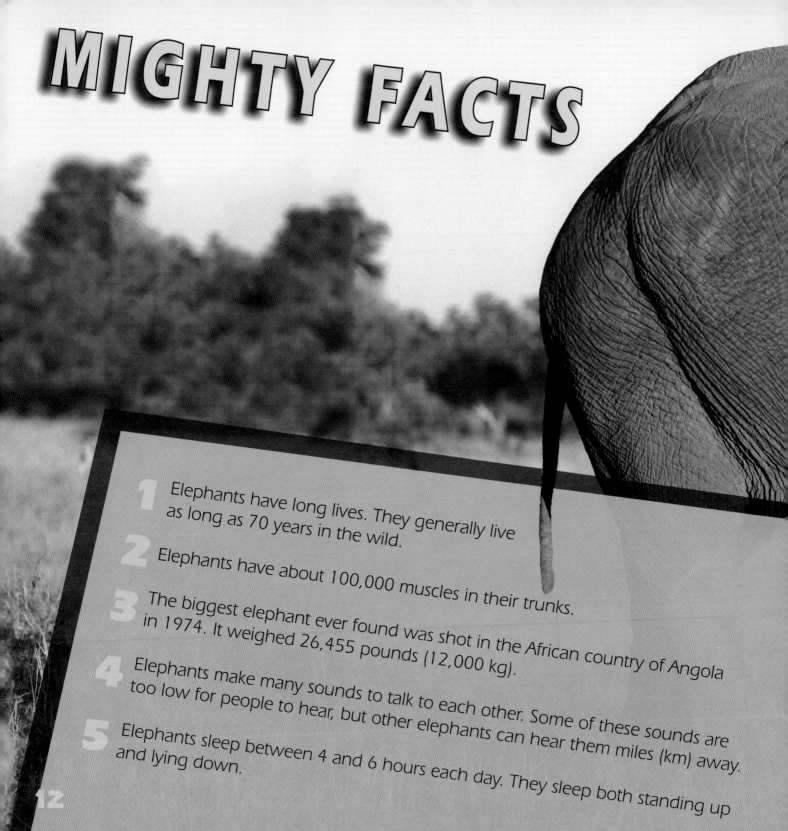

MIGHTY FACTS

1 Elephants have long lives. They generally live as long as 70 years in the wild.

2 Elephants have about 100,000 muscles in their trunks.

3 The biggest elephant ever found was shot in the African country of Angola in 1974. It weighed 26,455 pounds (12,000 kg).

4 Elephants make many sounds to talk to each other. Some of these sounds are too low for people to hear, but other elephants can hear them miles (km) away.

5 Elephants sleep between 4 and 6 hours each day. They sleep both standing up and lying down.

6 In dry weather, African bush elephants use their tusks to dig holes at the bottoms of dried-up rivers to find water.

7 Elephants are so strong that they can push trees over or pull them out of the ground in their search for food.

8 A savanna elephant's tusks often grow to be 8 feet (2 m) long.

Mothers in Charge

All kinds of elephants are **social**. They spend at least part of their lives in small herds, forming close ties to other elephants. Elephant herds are made up of adult female elephants and their children. Fully-grown male elephants live on their own most of the time.

The members of a herd are almost always related to each other. Herds are led by the oldest female elephants. These wise grandmothers lead their herds across many miles (km) in search of food and water. They learned the best eating and drinking spots from their own mothers. Elephants have good **memories**.

African elephant herds, such as this one, often walk between 2.5 and 7 miles (4–11 km) each day searching for food.

Cute Calves

Adult male elephants visit elephant herds to **mate** with females. Between 20 and 22 months after two elephants have mated, the female gives birth to a baby. Baby elephants are called calves. Calves are **clumsy** at first, but the other herd members teach them and care for them. Calves drink their mothers' milk to live.

Female elephants generally stay with the same herd their whole lives. Young male elephants live in their mothers' herds. When males are about 13 years old, they go off on their own. Some of these elephants gather with other young males to form groups, called bachelor herds.

Elephant calves, such as the one shown here, generally weigh between 117 and 330 pounds (53–150 kg) at birth.

Big Eaters

Elephants eat only plants. They eat many kinds and different parts of plants, such as grass, fruits, and leaves. African elephants use their tusks to tear the **bark** from trees to eat, too. People often think elephants eat and drink through their trunks, but this is not true. Elephants use their trunks to pick up food and water and bring it to their mouths.

It takes many plants to feed an animal as big as an elephant! Elephants eat between 220 and 400 pounds (100–181 kg) of food every day. They need lots of land to find enough food to eat.

An African elephant is shown here using its powerful trunk to pull on leaves and branches.

Who Would Hunt an Elephant?

A full-grown elephant is so big and powerful that it has no natural **predators**. However, there are a few animals that eat elephant calves. Lions and crocodiles hunt young African elephants. In Asia, elephants have to be on the lookout for tigers.

When predators try to catch elephant calves, the adult elephants in a herd will form a circle around the young elephants to keep them safe. Elephants will also care for any herd member that is sick. When there is danger, elephants will charge at predators. Elephants trumpet, or make a very loud sound, as they charge.

Lions are skilled hunters. They move through the tall savanna grasses in search of animals to kill.

Elephants in Danger

The biggest danger elephants face comes from people. People have taken over much of the land where elephants once lived to build homes, farms, and businesses. People also kill elephants for their tusks. Elephant tusks are made of **ivory**. People make figures and **jewelry** from ivory. In many countries, it is against the law to hunt elephants. However, hunters called poachers kill elephants anyway to sell their ivory.

Today, people are trying to keep elephants safe. Many countries have set land aside for them. Groups are working to stop poachers. Hopefully, we will always share our world with these gentle giants.

GLOSSARY

bark (BAHRK) The outside of the woody part of a tree.

clumsy (KLUM-zee) Slow or not skilled in movement.

ivory (EYEV-ree) The matter that makes up the extra long teeth of certain animals.

jewelry (JOO-ul-ree) Objects worn on the body.

mammals (MA-mulz) Warm-blooded animals that breathe air and feed milk to their young.

mate (MAYT) To come together to make babies.

memories (MEM-reez) The things that humans and animals remember.

predators (PREH-duh-terz) Animals that kill other animals for food.

savannas (suh-VA-nuz) Grasslands with few trees or bushes.

scientists (SY-un-tists) People who study the world.

social (SOH-shul) Living together in a group.

trunks (TRUNGKS) The extra long noses and upper lips of some animals.

INDEX

A
Africa, 6, 10
Asia, 6, 20

C
calves, 16, 20

F
farms, 22
food, 18
forests, 6
fruits, 18

G
grandmothers, 14
grass, 18

H
herd(s), 14, 16, 20

I
Indian elephants, 10
ivory, 22

L
land, 18
leaves, 18
lions, 20
logs, 6

M
mahouts, 6
muscles, 12

P
poachers, 22

S
savanna elephants, 6, 13
scientists, 4, 6
sound(s), 12, 20

T
Thailand, 6
tigers, 20
trees, 13
trunk(s), 4, 8, 12, 18
tusks, 13, 18

WEB SITES

Due to the changing nature of Internet links, PowerKids Press has developed an online list of Web sites related to the subject of this book. This site is updated regularly. Please use this link to access the list:
www.powerkidslinks.com/mamm/elephant/